ONE LAST TIME

GOOD-BYE TO YANKEE STADIUM

by Ray Negron
illustrated by Laura Seeley

Collins

An Imprint of HarperCollins *Publishers*

To my boss, George M. Steinbrenner III. You are always my inspiration.

To Laura Seeley, who has handled my "Steinbrenner-style demand"
for perfection with the skill of a da Vinci
and the result is the Mona Lisa of children's books.

To my staff
My chief of staff, Theresa Bunger
My man of many hats, Aris Sakellaridis
And my literary coach, Deni LaMarr
Without you it just doesn't work.

To my mother and father for letting me see the light.

To Chuck Feinstein
My only baseball coach. You prepared me for what was next, the Boss.
I'll miss you forever.

This book is dedicated to any person who has ever put on a baseball uniform—
Major League or Little League. Baseball will always be the people's game.

One Last Time: Good-bye to Yankee Stadium

Text copyright © 2009 by Ray Negron Illustrations copyright © 2009 by Laura Seeley Manufactured in China. All rights reserved. No part of this book may be used or reproduced in any manner whatsoever without written permission except in the case of brief quotations embodied in critical articles and reviews. For information address HarperCollins Children's Books, a division of HarperCollins Publishers, 1350 Avenue of the Americas, New York, NY 10019. www.harpercollinschildrens.com Library of Congress Cataloging-in-Publication Data is available. ISBN 978-0-06-147162-9 (trade bdg.) Designed by Stephanie Bart-Horvath 1 2 3 4 5 6 7 8 9 10 ❖ First Edition

FOREWORD

Yankee Stadium has always been a magical place. When I played at the stadium as a member of the Oakland A's, you just knew it. You could tell every time you walked onto that field that it was a field of dreams. I think I always played a little bit better there knowing I was on baseball's hallowed ground.

When Mr. Steinbrenner brought me to New York in 1977 and I got the opportunity to play in Yankee Stadium wearing pinstripes, there was a completely different feeling. You belonged to something unique—not only a part of baseball history but a part of a family, the Yankees.

That fall, in the World Series, I hit three home runs in Game 6 against the Dodgers and helped bring the World Series trophy back to New York. The late, great Thurman Munson gave me a nickname that I still answer to with pride today—Mr. October. It felt great to be a Yankee.

In the fall of 2008, the Yankees played their last game in Yankee Stadium. Like nearly everyone, I had mixed feelings about that. It hurt to see the old stadium go the way of the wrecking ball, but it is great to see a new generation of Yankees in a brand-new stadium.

The records and the moments will stand forever. Nobody is ever going to forget what Yankee Stadium has meant to the people of New York since it opened in 1923. Like the Babe, Lou, Joe D., Mickey and Roger, Thurman and Billy Martin, Yogi and all the rest, I am a part of that legacy. But it's time to move on. Guys like Jeter, Mariano, AROD, Robbie Cano, and all the others stand poised to make new memories.

The Yankees aren't going anywhere. The Bronx will always be their home, and they will always be playing at Yankee Stadium. In 2009, when they play the first Old-Timers' Day game in the new stadium, I will be proud to take my place along the base line with the rest of the Yankee family. It will be just like home.

—REGGIE JACKSON

 he game was over and the Yankees were in the locker room congratulating each other on another victory when the phone rang. Chien-Ming Wang picked it up.

"Hello? Hold on a second, Mr. Steinbrenner. He's here somewhere." He covered the receiver with his hand and called across the room. "Has anybody seen Ray, the batboy? There's a call for him. It's the Boss calling! Where's Ray?"

Ray walked into the room carrying a stack of Hideki Matsui's bats. "Here I am!" The bats clattered noisily as he dropped them onto the floor in front of Matsui's locker and took the phone.

"Hello? Yes sir, Boss, I'll be right up. I'm on the way!"

He hung up the phone and ran out of the locker room. AROD looked at Wang. "What do you think the Boss wants with Ray?"

Wang shrugged. "I don't know, but it sounded important."

ay was out of breath when he knocked on the door to the Boss's office.

"Come on in, Ray," said the Boss.

"Thanks," Ray said. He walked into the office and glanced around.

The Boss motioned to a chair. "Sit over here, Ray. Thanks for coming. I have a special assignment for you. I really need your help with this one."

As he sat, Ray leaned forward to listen. "Special assignment? Another sick kid, Boss? A kid who needs some special . . . magic?"

The Boss sighed. "Well, there's someone who needs some of your special magic, only this time it isn't a kid. This time it's me who needs your help."

The batboy gave him a worried look. "You? What's wrong, Boss?"

The Boss sounded serious. "Take a walk with me, Ray. We'll talk along the way."

They left his office and headed toward the field. "It's about the stadium, Ray. The old lady hasn't got many good years left in her. She's been standing for eighty-five years. Sometimes, more than fifty thousand people came to watch a game. Last year, we had more than four million fans here. It's very hard on the old lady handling those big crowds.

"In the old days, the crowds were even bigger," the Boss continued. "Did you know the Yankees once played a doubleheader against Boston and 81,841 people came?"

"Yep, sure did. May 30, 1938. The Yankees took two from the Red Sox. It was a great day for the boys in pinstripes," responded Ray.

The Boss smiled and patted him on the back. "That's my batboy! You really do know your Yankee history!"

"I've learned a lot from you, Boss!" Ray said proudly.

They walked onto the field and headed to the pitchers mound. The Boss stood there, slowly turning in a circle as he looked at the empty stadium from the same place where great Yankee pitchers stood. "This stadium has seen a lot, Ray. Twenty-six World Series Championships. Thirty-nine American League pennants. Presidents and even three popes were here. John Philip Sousa marched the 1922 pennant in here on the first day, April 18, 1923. That must have been something! I only wish I could have gotten the King to perform here."

"The King?" asked Ray.

"Elvis," said the Boss. "What a night that would have been! There are a lot of good memories, Ray. I've tried to spruce up the old lady, but all the wear and tear has taken its toll on her, and now I'm afraid we have to tear her down. She's falling apart."

ay looked shocked. "Tear down Yankee Stadium? You can't! Where will the Yankees play?"

"We're building a new stadium," said the Boss. "And it's going to be the greatest stadium baseball's ever seen. A stadium truly fit for the Yankees and their fans."

Tears formed in Ray's eyes. "You can build another stadium, but it won't be the same! It won't be Yankee Stadium anymore! What about the history? And the magic?"

"That's what I wanted to talk to you about, Ray," he said.

The Boss turned toward center field, stared at Monument Park, and sighed deeply. "Those great players, Ray. Those are the ones I'm concerned about. The ones who came before us. Babe Ruth for starters. Then Joe DiMaggio and the Mick, and Lou Gehrig, Bill Dickey, and Munson. All of them. They're part of the history of Yankee Stadium and I want them to know what we're doing."

The Boss turned to Ray and patted him on the back. "That's going to be your job, Ray. And it's a big one—the biggest job I've ever asked you to do. I want you to let them know Yankee pride and tradition are going to continue, but they are going to have a new home and they're invited to be part of it. We're not leaving any of them behind. We're moving the monuments to a new Monument Park. Those are some of the greatest guys who ever played the game of baseball, and they'll go wherever we go.

"It's going to be a hard job, Ray. Tell them the old lady is coming down and they can come here one last time and say good-bye. Do you think you can do it?"

ay stared at the numbers on the wall in Monument Park as he wiped the tears from his eyes. Every one of those numbers represented someone very special in the hearts of Yankee fans. They were the Yankee greats he had heard about when he was growing up. He knew their history by heart. Yankee Stadium was home and he didn't want to leave it, but he knew the Boss was right.

"Yes, Boss! I'll find them and bring them here. They should have a chance to see Yankee Stadium one last time."

The Boss smiled and put his arm around Ray's shoulder. "I knew you would help. Now, let's go back to the locker room. I want to tell the guys before the press conference tomorrow. They deserve to be the first to know."

he building of the new stadium began on schedule. As Ray sat in the dugout, his gaze often went out to the left-field wall and the steel structure rising behind it. Sometimes tears filled his eyes and he had to look away. Every day brought him closer and closer to when it would be time to say good-bye to his old home and move on.

Then, one fine spring day, the Boss found Ray straightening out bats and helmets for the players.

"It's time, Ray," he said. "They're tearing her down. The new stadium is ready. It's time to say good-bye. I know it's hard for you, but can you do it?"

"Yes," Ray said. "I have to. If I don't tell them, who will?"

When the players were done with their workout, they looked for Ray, but he was gone. They were too busy getting ready for the big opening day to worry about him, anyway. They were going to play in a brand-new stadium. They joked about whether Jeter would hit the first home run and if Chien-Ming Wang would get the first win. It was a new chapter in the Yankees' history book.

Ray was worried. He had managed to find everyone on the list—Billy Martin, Joe DiMaggio, Mickey and Roger, Catfish Hunter and Thurman Munson. He even found the Babe. But as hard as he tried, he couldn't seem to find Lou Gehrig. Time was running out. Lou just had to be there. It wouldn't be the same without him.

"What should I do?" he asked the Babe. "I can't find Lou anywhere! The Boss said to make sure all of you were there. Where can Lou be?"

The Babe thought for a moment. "I know," he said. "Follow me—he's over here!"

Ray breathed a sigh of relief. At last, he'd found everyone on his list.

The next morning, Ray opened the shutter that led to the magic room. Standing there were some of the Yankee legends: Mickey Mantle, Roger Maris, Thurman Munson, and many others. They stepped out into the hallway. The Babe and Lou were the last ones to leave the room.

"Right this way, and hurry!" Ray said. "Your lockers and equipment are ready."

The players smiled at the batboy.

"You think of everything, Ray," Thurman said.

"That's why he's the batboy," said Billy. "Best batboy I ever had, too."

It's great to be back at Yankee Stadium," said Elston Howard, putting on his catcher's mask.

"Yeah, but Ray told me they're tearing it down," replied the Babe glumly.

"It isn't right to tear down our stadium!" Mickey said sadly. "Think of all that history, gone with the wrecking ball!" He shook his head and sighed.

"Sometimes change is good," replied Lou. "You have to let go so the new guys have their chance to become heroes. We had our turn. The stadium's just too old. I hear the new one's nice."

"Yes," said Mickey, "but what about all the records set here? All the games we played? Don't they matter anymore?"

"I don't know," added Roger. "Ray told me the new stadium's the best in baseball. Besides, records are made to be broken."

"Right." The Babe grinned as he looked at Roger. "Like the way you broke mine with sixty-one homers in sixty-one?" Everyone laughed. "I was proud of you that day, Roger. I was proud to be a Yankee."

"What about your record, Lou?" asked Mickey. "You were the Iron Horse, 2,130 consecutive games! It's broken now, too."

"Ripken earned it, Mickey," said Lou. "He worked hard and never gave up. Roger's right. Records should be broken. I was proud when I heard."

"That's what baseball's all about—doing your best and never giving up," Casey Stengel added.

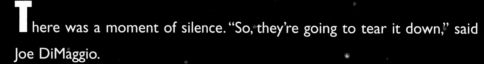

There was a moment of silence. "So, they're going to tear it down," said Joe DiMaggio.

Thurman nodded. "I'm ready to get behind the plate one more time, spit in my catcher's mitt, pound it in good, and catch a fastball out over the plate."

"I'm ready to throw it to you," said Catfish.

"Hey, Mickey? Remember when you hit the facade?" asked the Babe. "Heck of a shot. Nobody ever hit one out of the park here, but you came close."

"I hit the facade two or three times, Babe." Mickey smiled proudly. "Remember the Murderers' Row team? You hit sixty home runs that year."

The Babe chuckled. "Who doesn't remember that?"

"Think you can hit that sixtieth again, Babe?" Mickey asked.

"I can if you can hit that facade again," challenged the Babe.

"I want to stand in center field one last time," said DiMaggio. "I bet I can still hear the crowd cheering. What a great sound that was."

"You've got a record that still stands, Joe," said Billy. "The fifty-six-game hitting streak. They call that the record that'll never be broken."

Joe shook his head. "I don't know, Billy. They have kids on the team now who have a good shot at it. One of these days, somebody will break it."

"Players today are different," said Elston. "Do you know they got kids just out of short pants who throw a hundred miles per hour?"

"No kidding!" said Bill Dickey. "Imagine catching one of those!"

"So, what do you say, guys? Is everybody ready to get out there and play one last time?" asked Lefty Gomez.

"Sure! Let's do it!" yelled Mickey.

Everyone ran out onto the field. The sun was shining on a warm spring afternoon. The players happily ran the bases and slid into home plate. Some played catch in the outfield, and others picked up bats and took practice swings.

Billy was wearing his uniform with his famous cowboy boots. He stood on the top step of the dugout with Casey.

"I'm sure as heck going to have a hard time putting together a lineup, Billy," Casey said. "If I start Munson, Bill Dickey will be mad at me. If I start Dickey, Elston will be mad. Ah well, it's always my fault."

"It always was, Casey," said Billy, laughing.

Casey chuckled. "Well, we'll start by putting you at second base. Now get out there!"

"Okay, but who do we have to play shortstop?"

"I'm glad you asked," Casey said. "I just brought up a new guy. Remember Phil Rizzuto?"

Phil ran up the dugout stairs with a huge grin on his face. He patted Billy on the back. "Come on, you huckleberry, we need some infield practice."

"Right behind you, Scooter!" Billy said as he jogged onto the field in his boots.

Thurman crouched behind the plate, then spit into his glove and pounded it again.

Lefty walked out to the mound and threw some warm-up tosses.

Phil looked around at the famous facade and glanced up at the broadcasting booth. "Holy cow, I made it!" he said.

The Boss came down the stairs and took a seat next to the dugout. His eyes darted back and forth across the field, not quite believing all the famous players gathered together to play one last game on the old field.

The Babe walked up to the plate, pointed to the outfield, and repeated his famous home run. As the Babe trotted around the bases, Roger Maris waited at home plate to shake his hand.

ext, Bill Dickey caught and Catfish Hunter pitched. Roger came up to bat and hit a home run to right field—just like his record-breaking sixty-first. The other players cheered wildly. When he touched home plate, the Babe was there to give him a high five.

The Babe took a turn pitching to Elston. Joe hit next, a double right between Lou at first and Billy at second. Thurman followed with a hard single. Mickey made a good throw from center field and Joe stopped at third. Phil got up to the plate and laid down a perfect bunt that rolled down the first-base line, just staying fair. Joe scored, sliding into home plate and raising a huge cloud of dust as his teammates cheered. It was just like the old days. Ray sat in the dugout with Casey and the Boss, watching the players relive the famous plays. He couldn't believe it was happening right before his eyes.

The sun started to sink in the sky and the air turned colder as Mickey stepped up to the plate. The Babe let one go and Mickey swung hard. The ball sailed into the sun and smacked hard against the facade. At just that moment, bricks and mortar scattered across center field. A piece of the facade fell to the ground. The loud hum of bulldozers began. The players looked at one another and began to run.

Ray hurried out of the dugout. "Roger! Mickey! Hurry! It's time to go! We have to say good-bye now. We have to go back to the magic room before it's gone or you won't be able to leave!"

The Boss ran onto the field waving his cell phone. "We have to hurry, Ray! I just got word. It's coming down now! Look out!"

Bricks began to rain down from above them. Large pieces of the famous white facade slammed onto the outfield grass.

"Well, I'm not ruining this new pair of cowboy boots!" shouted Billy as he led the players off the field.

abe! Lou! This way! Watch out!" the Boss cried. He ran toward the dugout, but he stumbled and fell on the way.

Ray turned around with terror in his eyes. "Boss?" He started to run to help.

The Babe and Lou reached the Boss first and helped him up. "We have him, Ray!" called Lou.

"Get everyone into the room. You have to lead the way. We're right behind you!" the Babe shouted.

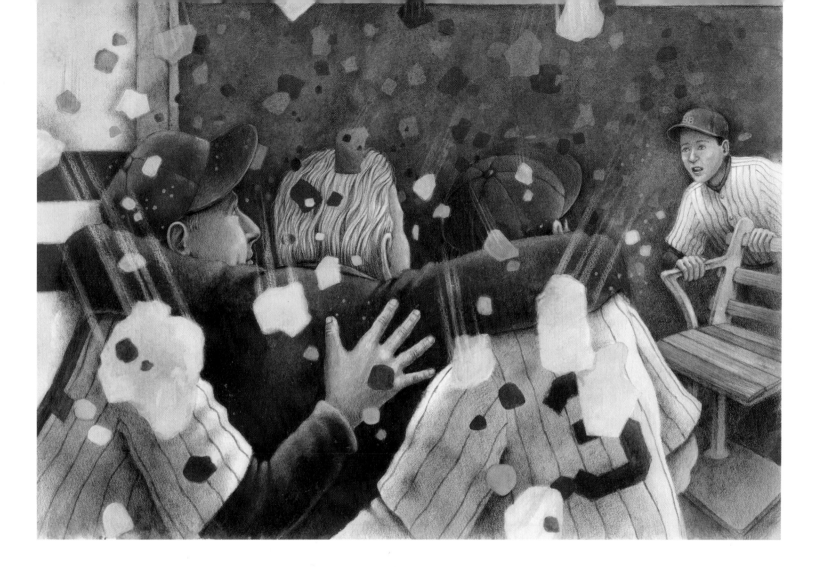

Ray headed toward the magic room, with the players following him. When he got there, he pulled the shutter open and, one by one, the players entered the room, thanking Ray for bringing them together one last time. The walls of the stadium were starting to shake. Ray began to panic. Where were the Babe and Lou? Where was the Boss? Would they make it in time?

Finally, Ray heard them running down the hall. The Babe and Lou rushed into the room, pausing long enough to turn around for one final look.

t still isn't right, tearing down the House that Ruth Built," said the Babe.

"Sure it is, Babe," Lou said. "You have to make room for the new guys and think about the future. We had our time in the sun. We heard the cheers—and the boos, too. We stood and watched proudly as pennants were raised over the stadium. None of us will ever forget how it felt to be a Yankee. And they'll never forget us, Babe. They might tear down the House that Ruth Built, but we're still the Yankees, and every kid who ever puts on pinstripes will know about us." Lou looked around the special room one last time, then put his arm around the Babe. "Come on, it's time to go. Trust me, Babe, the fans will remember."

The Boss stood with his hand on Ray's shoulder. "You can count on that. Nobody's ever going to forget you. Watching you play made me even prouder of the new stadium. It's a memorial to all of you. The greatest Yankees who ever played the game! Brought together one last time by Ray and his special magic."

The Babe tipped his cap. "Good luck with the new stadium," he said. "If you don't mind, with Ray's help, maybe I'll poke my head in now and then to see how the new kids are doing."

"Maybe I will, too," added Lou.

The Boss smiled. "It'll be a pleasure to have you. You're part of the Yankee family and always will be." There were tears of pride in the eyes of the Babe and Lou.

 he Babe and Lou stood arm in arm as the Boss reached up to close the shutter. Ray could feel the tears streaming down his face as he watched. Just as the shutter started to cover their faces, he raced forward.

"Wait, guys! Take me with you, Babe! I want to go with you. Please, Lou?"

The Boss grabbed him and held him back. "You can't go, Ray. You have to stay here. I need you."

"Boss, I have to go with them! What about the magic? Let me go!" Ray said, struggling to get free.

The Boss held him tightly and spoke. "Don't worry about the magic, Ray. We're taking it with us. The Yankees will always have that magic."

"But I want to go with them!" Ray said through his tears.

"Not your time, Ray. There are still too many things for you to do down here," said the Boss as he wrapped his arm around his batboy's shoulder. "That's just the way life is, Ray. We have to move on. . . ."

"The Boss is right, Ray. We had our time. This is yours," said the Babe.

"Listen to Babe," said Lou. "You're Ray, the batboy. It's your job."

Ray wiped the tears from his face. "Okay. I love you, Babe, and you, too, Lou. You make me proud to be a Yankee. I'll never forget a single minute of today."

"Neither one of us will," said the Boss. "God bless you boys."

Lou and the Babe tipped their caps. "You, too, Boss."

Ray stepped forward and grabbed the shutter. He looked at the Boss, who nodded to him. Together, Ray and the Boss lowered the shutter one last time. "Come on, Ray," said the Boss. "It's time to go home. To our new home."

AN OPEN LETTER TO THE YANKEE GREATS

This is a letter to everyone who has ever worn a Yankee uniform and played at Yankee Stadium. In my mind you are all greats—a part of the rich history that has produced more championships than any team in the history of sports. So this is for the Babe, Lou, Elston, all of you. . . .

When I was a kid, I used to go up to Yankee Stadium late at night when they were cleaning the stadium after the game. I was going through a lot in my life, and the stadium was my place to let go of some of the pressure. It was then that I discovered you.

I have a message for you from the Boss. No matter which side of the street Yankee Stadium is on, we still need you with us. You are our guides from the past into the future. We still need Catfish to whisper a tip into a young pitcher's ear about how to grip the ball when throwing a curve. We still need Scooter's bunting hints. We still need Billy Martin teaching our guys how to play Billyball. We still need to know that you are with us in spirit, helping to make the Yankees great.

You who have gone before us need to know that the new stadium is still Yankee Stadium—the greatest sports venue in the universe. We'll be waiting for you across the street. You'll know how to find the way—just follow the crowds. We'll be waiting for you.

—RAY NEGRON